First published in paperback in 2003
Published by
Evans Brothers Limited
2A Portman Mansions
Chiltern Street
London W1U 6NR

First published 1999
Reprinted 2001, 2003

Series editor: Su Swallow
Illustrations and page design: Tim Scrivens, T J Graphics
Production: Jenny Mulvanny

Printed in Hong Kong by Wing King Tong Co. Ltd

Good, Keith
Exciting electrics. – (Design challenge)
1. Electric engineering – Juvenile Literature
I. Title II. Scrivens, Tim
621.3

ISBN 0 237 52539 9

For details of initial teacher training and in-service courses in
Design Technology at the University of Greenwich, contact
Keith Good by fax +44 (0)208 331 9504 or e-mail
k.w.good@gre.ac.uk

Acknowledgments

For permission to reproduce copyright material the authors
and publishers gratefully acknowledge the following:

page 6 Jerry Mason, Science Photo Library **page 8** Reg
Watson, Tony Stone Worldwide **page 10** Phil Degginger,
Tony Stone Images **page 12** Food and Drug Administration,
Science Photo Library **page 14** Don Smetzer, Tony Stone
Images **page 16** Last Resort Picture Library **page 20** Nick
Dolding, Tony Stone Images **page 22** Last Resort Picture
Library **page 24** Last Resort Picture Library **page 26** Last
Resort Picture Library

VISIT OUR WEBSITE
www.evansbooks.co.uk

DESIGN CHALLENGE

Exciting Electrics

Keith Good

Evans

About this book

About this series

This series involves children in designing and making their own working technology projects, using readily available salvaged or cheap materials. Each project is based on a 'recipe' that promotes success and crucially, stimulates the reader's own ideas. The 'recipes' also provide a good introduction to important technology in everyday life. The projects can be developed to different levels of sophistication according to the reader's ability and can reflect their other interests. The series teaches skills and knowledge in a fun way and encourages creative, innovative ideas.

About this book

One reason for giving children hands-on experience of electrics is that they are surrounded by electrical devices every day and practical experience helps them to understand their world better. This book focuses on making a range of battery-powered projects with an emphasis on fun, creativity and readily available materials. The ideas can also be used to enhance other design projects, perhaps based on mechanisms e.g. lights for a new fairground ride.

It is a good idea to observe the convention of RED wire for positive (+) and BLACK wire for negative (-) as some components will only work if connected the right way round. When working with groups of children, one or two batteries can be used by all to test their projects. Limiting the number of batteries saves cost - and reduces the noise from buzzers! Agreeing to keep the batteries in fixed places saves searching.

Safety

● Children must be made to understand that mains electricity can be lethal and that they must never tamper with it. This should in any case be part of their general 'keeping safe' education but always stressed when introducing electrics. All projects in this book use battery power only.

● Children must not use rechargeable batteries. These give up a lot of energy (heat) quickly if short circuited e.g. if a paperclip bridges the two terminals.

● Adult use of craft knives is strongly advised. These must be used with a cutting board (or mat) and a safety rule with a groove to protect the fingers. Card is often best cut for children on a paper trimmer with a guarded wheel cutter. A sharp paper trimmer is a good way to cut foil strips for children.

● Use wire strippers not craft knives to remove the plastic insulation from wires. If possible, get children to try (and evaluate) different types of wire stripper before buying one.

Contents

Electric circuits

Making series and parallel circuits

It is hard to imagine the world around us without electric power. We use it to cook our food and to keep it cool, it lights our homes and powers our computers and toys. How many other uses for electricity can you think of?

The activities on these two pages will help you with the projects in this book.

Safety

Remember that the projects in this book are all powered by batteries. The mains electricity that comes from the sockets in your house is much too powerful and could kill you. Use battery power only!

You will need

● a battery and battery snap (connector)
● 2 6-volt bulbs and bulb holders
● Some multi-strand wire (the kind with lots of thin wires inside the plastic)
● a wire-stripping tool
● a small screwdriver

What to do

1. Screw the bulb into a bulb holder.

2. Use your screwdriver to join the battery wires to the bulb holder. Loosen the screws and make a loop of wire round them before tightening again.

3. Connect the battery and the bulb will light.

Electricity is flowing from the battery through the wires and bulb and back to the battery. You have made a *series circuit*.

A series circuit

battery

connector

bulb and bulb holder

The series circuit you have made can be drawn like this:

battery   bulb

wire

4. Undo one of the wires joined to the bulb. What happens?

A complete 'loop' is needed for a circuit to work. A switch is a gap in a circuit that can be closed easily to turn things on. All the switches in this book work by closing a gap in a circuit.

5. Try adding another bulb to your series circuit to see what difference this makes.

To join the bulbs, cut some wire with the wire stripper and remove the plastic insulation from each end.

6. Now try making a *parallel circuit* (see below). Are the bulbs brighter or dimmer than before? A parallel circuit will be needed when your project includes more than one bulb, buzzer or motor.

A series circuit with two bulbs

A parallel circuit

The series circuit with two bulbs can be drawn like this:

The parallel circuit you have made can be drawn like this:

Light, sound and movement

Designing circuits for your projects

Electrical and electronic parts are often called *components*. Many different components are used in the personal stereos, computer games and other products we see every day. The microchip (see photograph, right), used in computers and many other devices, is one component that has changed our lives.

Here are some simpler components that you can use in circuits and design projects.

Light

Bulbs are useful when you want quite bright lights or to light something up. You can make them even brighter by making a reflector (which torches and headlamps use) out of foil. Bulbholders are quite bulky but can often be hidden inside a project leaving the bulb showing.

LEDs (light emitting diodes) are the small red, green or yellow lights on computers, phones and many other products. How many LEDs can you find in your home? LEDs are cheap, colourful and give projects a 'high tech' look.

The short leg of the LED must be joined to the black (*negative* −) wire. The flat part of the LED is always next to the short leg. Join the long leg to the red (*positive* +) wire.

LEDs can cope with 3 volts but if using a 9-volt (9v) battery you must add a resistor or the LED will be ruined. You need a resistor called 200 ohm. It can be joined to either leg.

bulb

bulb holder

resistor

symbol for LED

LED

Sound

Round buzzers and rectangular buzzers sound different! The red wire from the buzzer must be joined to the red wire from the battery. The black wire from the buzzer must be joined to the black wire from the battery.

You can use a capacitor to make a buzzer or light stay on for a short time (then fade) after the switch goes off. The capacitor must be connected the right way round. Look for the negative (-) markings which show you where to join the black wire from the battery.

Buzzers

symbol for buzzer

Capacitors

symbol for capacitor

Movement

pulleys

Motor

Motors often turn too fast but not strongly enough for many projects. Pulleys or gears are added to reduce the speed and increase the force of the motor.

To do useful work motors need to be fixed in place with stick-on clips.

symbol for motor

M

stick-on clip

Tip

Bulb holders and buzzers can be fixed to your work with plastic bag ties or single strand wire.

Getting ideas

You could design and model your own electronic product of the future – it doesn't really have to work! Make a list of battery-powered products to help you get ideas. Look at battery-powered products and, **with adult help**, look inside broken, unwanted ones.

Shopping catalogues and visits to shops will also give you ideas for your own designs. You could include some of the components on these two pages and control them with switches from this book.

More about making circuits
Joining wires and adding switches

Circuits only work when the parts are joined properly. Solder – a mixture of tin and lead – can be melted between the parts, using a hot soldering iron. This makes a good strong joint that conducts electricity well, but soldering can be dangerous. Here are some other ways to make your circuits.

Multi-strand wire

1. Use wires with lots of strands. They are easiest to twist together tightly. Strip off about 1cm of the insulation first. Putting tape over the joins can help to keep them together and prevents accidental electrical connections.

2. Although connecting strip is bulky, it can be a useful way to join parts. Cut off what you need and fix the wires with a screwdriver.

Connecting strip

Where you put your switch decides which components it will control. If the switch is put in this position, it controls both components.

3. Making a circuit on a board can help you to see what you are doing and avoid mistakes. Stick the wires down with masking tape and test your circuit before fixing it into a project. Remember to make the wires long enough.

A switch symbol can be drawn like this

If the switch is put here one component will be on all the time and the other can be turned on and off.

This is where to put a capacitor (see page 9) so that the buzzer stays on for a while and gradually fades after the switch is off.

capacitor

Here both switches must be on before the circuit will work. One switch (like a pressure pad switch, page 12 or reed switch, page 24) could be hidden to work like a secret key.

When a magnet is passed over the reed switch (page 24), the LEDs (see page 9) glow then slowly dim. The buzzer goes on and makes a wailing noise before going quiet. This circuit could be used to make a creature that comes to life when it is stroked.

Getting ideas

Try to think of different uses for the circuits shown on these pages. Draw some other circuits that you think would work. You could draw lifelike components or use symbols (see pages 8 and 9). Try the circuits out if you can.

If you can borrow different kinds of wire stripper try them out and compare them. Which do you prefer and why? **Safety**: some wire strippers have sharp parts so take care.

Tip

What to do if your circuit doesn't work:

● Check that the battery is working. Try it on a spare buzzer or light.

● Check that all the parts are in the right place and connected the right way round.

● If a circuit that used to work stops working, see if something has come loose.

Pressure pads
Making your own pressure pad switch

Pressure pad switches (sometimes called membrane panel switches) are made from thin layers. They are tough and don't take up much room. Look for pressure pads on cash point machines, microwave ovens and other machines that we use every day.

You can make a pressure pad switch to control anything that is battery-powered.

kitchen foil

staple

You will need

- 3 pieces of card (postcard size)
- scissors
- a glue stick
- a stapler
- kitchen foil
- something to switch on e.g. bulb, buzzer, LED (see page 9 for help)

What to do

1. Cut a hole in one piece of card like the one in the picture (page 12). This will be in the middle layer.

2. Use the hole to stencil a square on the top and bottom layers.

3. Stick a square of foil over the square on the top layer.

4. Stick two strips of foil *across* the square on the bottom layer.

5. Staple your switch together at one edge like a book.

6. Staple the bare wires tightly to the foil strips - and try it!

Getting ideas

How many ways are there to turn a pressure pad on? Think about the following questions to help you get ideas. Could you swing something at it, put it where it would be turned on by accident, sit on it, or roll something over it? Could you drop something on it, stand on it, press it with your finger or do something else?

What could you turn on with a battery-powered pressure pad – a light bulb, an electric motor, an LED, a buzzer or something else?

Could you design a creature with eyes that glow when you stroke its back? Could you make a burglar alarm? Try a bigger switch so that a foot makes it go on, and use thicker card. If you put the switch under a model road layout, toy cars could turn it on – or make up a target game like this one!

Tip

If your switch stays on, try a smaller hole.

A simple pressure pad game
Some ideas to get you started

One way to use your pressure pad (see page 12) is to make a simple board game. A treasure hunt, for example, could lead to the magic spot by a series of clues, and a light or buzzer would come on when a player landed in the right square.

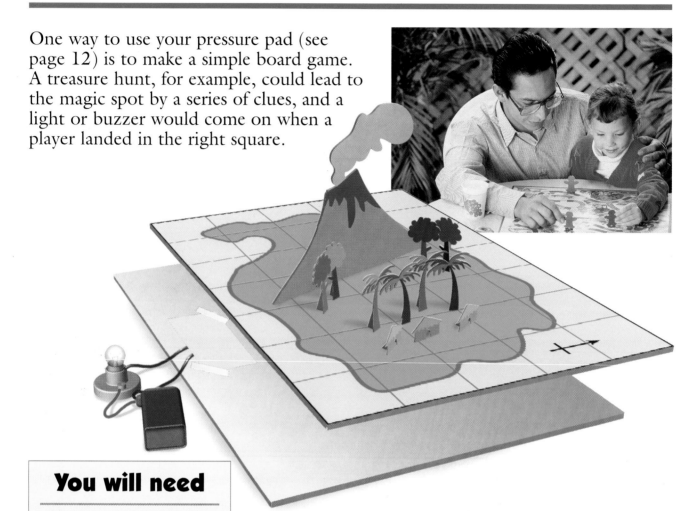

You will need

- a pressure pad with light or buzzer connected (see page 12)
- 2 sheets of card
- masking tape or coloured pvc tape
- colouring pencils and markers

You could also use:
- words and pictures done on a computer
- rub-on letters
- coloured stickers

What to do

1. Make a pressure pad with a light or buzzer connected (see page 12).

2. Fix the pressure pad to one of the sheets of card. Use masking tape or PVC tape so that you can move the pad to different places. How could this make the game more interesting?

3. Before adding your game design to the top layer of card, find the sensitive spot and mark it with a pencil. You may need to add longer wires to your switch if making a large game.

You can add more pressure pad switches to make a game with extra sensitive places.

In this picture the bulb will light up if either of the pressure pad switches is pressed.

connecting strip

Tip

Hinge the two pieces of card with tape or staples so that you can reach inside.

Getting ideas

You could use a pressure pad switch in a game. Look at games that already exist. Talk to older people about games they used to play. Find out about games from different countries. All this might help you to design your own games – but don't just copy!

Think about who will play the game. How difficult should it be to play? Try to make up rules that are fair and easy to understand. If you can, use a computer to type out the rules.

Could you make counters or other extras? You might use painted pebbles, card figures or salt dough shapes. You could make packaging and advertising for your game.

More pressure pad games

Pressure pads with several sensitive places

Pressure pad panels on cash points, microwave ovens and other products often have lots of sensitive places.

Here is how to make your own pressure pad with several sensitive places. When any of these places are pressed your circuit will be turned on. You can use your pad to make more complicated games.

You will need

- 3 sheets of thin card, A4 size
- craft knife, safety ruler and cutting board
  Safety note: check with an adult before using a craft knife
- kitchen foil
- glue stick
- circuit to switch on
- stapler

What to do

1. Draw a grid on one sheet of card (use faint pencil lines as you may not want the lines to show later). This sheet will be the top layer.

2. Cover the underside of the top layer with foil apart from a strip at one end.

3. Look at 'Getting ideas' (page 17) and design your game or quiz. Decide which squares you want to be switches and mark them in pencil. You don't have to choose the ones in the picture – choose as many as you want.

4. Draw the same grid on the middle layer. Mark the same squares as you marked on the top layer and cut them out.

top layer

middle layer

12 x 2 cm squares

10 x 2 cm squares

5. Cover the bottom layer with foil apart from a strip at one end.

6. Staple on the circuit. Staple the pieces of card together so they open like a book.

Important: staple through the bare strips of card or the staples will conduct electricity and your switch will stay on!

staple card together here

staple circuit

Tip

If your switch stays on when it shouldn't be add an extra layer with 'windows' or add pieces of card with smaller windows.

Getting ideas

Design a game using the pad you have made. You could look at games like snakes and ladders and design your own version. You could draw the hazards (like monsters) on the sensitive squares or leave them unmarked to surprise the players! The switch squares could show hidden treasure instead of hazards and dangers. Use your pad to design a quiz for younger children. Write or draw pictures showing the right answers on the sensitive squares. Show wrong answers on squares where there are no switches. By covering and uncovering some holes in the middle layer you could fool people who think they know where the switches are!

You could go on to design your own pads and think of your own uses for them.

A secret switch
A pressure pad with pairs of switches

Key pads are often used when only certain people are allowed to open a door. These people are told which numbers to press to open the door, and they keep the numbers secret. You can make a pressure pad where the circuit will only work by pressing the right two places at the same time.

10 × 2 cm squares

12 × 2 cm squares

middle layer

bottom layer

kitchen foil

top layer

What to do

1. Draw a grid on one sheet of card. This will be the middle layer. Cut out the squares shown.

2. Use the holes to stencil squares on the underside of the top layer. Also stencil the squares on the top surface of the bottom layer.

3. Cover the squares underneath the top layer with foil. Fix the foil with a glue stick. ⬆

Tip

Flip the 'stencil' to make sure that the squares are one above the other when the pad is put together.

If your switch stays on when it shouldn't be add an extra layer with 'windows' or add pieces of card with smaller windows.

middle layer

top layer

don't glue
under here

4. Use your middle layer as a stencil once more to mark the sensitive squares on the upper side of the top layer.

Important: check that the squares on the three layers are above each other when the pad is put together.

5. Add the foil tracks to the bottom layer as shown in the picture below.

Make the six gaps about 3mm wide. These are the switches.

Important: don't glue where the tracks cross – this may act as an insulator.

6. Staple on the circuit as shown. Staple the pad together so that it opens like a book.

Press both the switches in the bottom row, then try the other pairs.

Getting ideas

You could design a quiz where two things have to be matched, e.g. animals with their homes, sports players with their country or team. Put a pair of answers over each pair of switches. Put wrong answers over the rest of the sheet where there are no switches.

You could hide one of each pair of switches so that only you know how to turn the circuit on. Try to think of projects that use this idea.

Secret 'combination lock' switch
Making your own security device

To make this switch work you have to turn the top layer to the right position and know where to press. Only those who know the secret can make the circuit work. All around you can see electronic ways of letting one person make something happen while stopping others. Your library card has its own special bar code. Credit and cash point cards have their own magnetic strip and number. Special cameras can scan your eye to check that it's really you.

You can use this switch as a security device to decide who can turn on projects, or to make puzzles, games and quizzes.

You will need

- 2 pieces of A4 card
- kitchen foil
- paper fastener
- circuit

What to do

1. Cut a 15cm wide strip of card and fold it in half. Cut another piece to fit on top.

2. Cut a 2cm square 'window' in the strip and use the hole to stencil a square on the other two layers.

3. Stick foil over the square on the top layer. Stick two strips across the bottom square. (They should be close together but not touching.)

4. Draw the largest circle that will fit on the top layer and cut it out.

5. Staple the circuit to the foil strips. Fix the top and middle layers together with a paper fastener. Turn the circle to the right place and press!

You can develop the basic switch idea by adding extra card disks with 'windows' cut in them. All the windows must be lined up before the circuit will work. Make each disk slightly smaller than the one below it so that you can turn them easily.

Tip

You can add more foil squares to the top layers of these switches if you want extra 'on' positions.

Getting ideas

You could use the switch like a combination lock. Think of different things it could control. Could it control a motor that pulled back a catch? Could you make a 'doorbell' that only friends would know how to work?

Think about using the switch in puzzles, games and quizzes. You could put pictures around the disk. When the correct picture on the disk is lined up with its name, the switch would work. On the second version of the switch you could ask the player to line up all the pictures that go together before they press.

Try out your switch – it may help you have other ideas.

The push-to-break switch

A switch that is always on – unless you press it!

A switch that is on all the time unless it is pressed is called a push-to-break switch because you push it to 'break' (make a gap in) a circuit. You probably have one (or more) in your home. One use for this kind of switch is to control the light inside refrigerators. When the door is shut it pushes on a switch, breaks the circuit and keeps the light off, which saves energy. Here's how to make a push-to-break switch and other kinds of switches to use in design projects.

You will need

- piece of plastic bottle
- some kitchen foil
- glue stick
- stapler
- small piece of card

A push-to-break switch
Press to switch OFF.

What to do

1. Cut two strips of plastic 2cm wide and 6cm long.

Stick foil to both sides using the glue stick.

2. Bend the strips into the shapes shown.

3. Stick the strips to the card, making sure that they spring together until the bottom one is pressed.

4. Staple the circuit to the strips – it should stay on until you press the switch!

You can change the switch so that you have to press to turn the circuit on. Just pull one part above the other and you have a push-to-make switch. Can you see the difference between this switch and the first one?

In a knife switch, one part of the knife switch is turned to make contact with the other when you want a circuit to stay on.

A push-to-make switch
Press to switch ON.

Knife switch

Getting ideas

Think of different ways to make the switches go on or off. You could leave something resting on the push-to-break switch. If anyone moves the object the circuit could warn you. Opening a lid or door could also make a circuit work.

The push-to-make switch could be used to signal with. You could find out about Morse code. You could use this switch as part of a pinball game or whenever you want a circuit to go on. How could you keep the push-to-make switch on?

You could use the knife switch when one of your projects needs a circuit that will stay on, like the lights on a model vehicle. A cotton thread could pull the knife switch on.

The reed switch

A switch that works without being touched!

The reed switch works when a magnet is brought near it. Reed switches are used to sound an alarm when a burglar opens a door or window. They have also been used where the spark from an ordinary switch would cause an explosion. These switches can be hidden under card, fabric or other material – as long as the magnetism can reach them they will still work.

Only a magnet will make the switch work!

You will need

- reed switch
- magnet
- 2 pieces of connecting strip
- small screwdriver
- circuit

What to do

1. Use the screwdriver to fix a piece of connecting strip to each end of the reed switch.

Safety: reed switches are made of glass so handle them with care. Don't bend their wires or you may crack them.

2. Add a circuit to the other ends of the connector strips.

3. Bring a magnet close to the switch to test your circuit. You may need to turn the switch or magnet to make it work well.

A strong magnet will turn on the switch from some distance away – experiment!

reed switch

To keep your reed switch in place on a project you could use tape, or plastic bag ties.

It is easier to put the magnet on the moving part of a project instead of the circuit. What would happen on this project (right) if the wheel with the magnet turned faster?

Tip

When using lights be careful not to leave the magnet near the switch by accident or you will waste your battery.

Getting ideas

There are many ways to move the magnet near the reed switch. It could be fixed to a wheel, swung on a thread, slid in a tube or be fixed under a toy car. Think of other ways to bring the magnet close to the switch. Do any of these give you ideas for design projects?

Hiding the magnet and switch might give you ideas for design projects. The magnet could be hidden by fixing it to your finger with clear tape or put inside a magic wand. You could design a creature with eyes that lit up only when you stroked it. Remember the reed switch is special because it doesn't have to be touched to make it work!

The tilt switch

A switch that works when something moves

When a ball rolls inside the tilt switch the circuit is turned on. A thief rocking a car could make the tilt switch set off an alarm. A pedometer (see photograph), which measures how far someone has walked, uses a tilt switch to count leg movements. Some tilt switches use a liquid metal called mercury. Others use a small metal ball. Here's how to make your own tilt switch and ideas to start you thinking about how to use it.

You will need

- 2 corks
- piece of plastic bottle to make the tube
- 2 paper clips (not coloured ones)
- clear tape
- small glass marble
- kitchen foil

What to do

1. Make a tube 10cm long by wrapping the plastic tightly round the corks. Hold the tube in shape with tape.

2. Wrap the marble tightly in the foil to make a round shape that will roll easily.

3. Twist the bare ends of your circuit tightly round the paper clips.

4. Tape the paper clips to a cork. Make them stick well out from the cork. Push the cork and paperclips into one end of the tube.

5. Put the marble in the tube. Check that it moves easily and touches both paperclips – switching the circuit on! (You may need to bend the paper clips in a little.)

6. Once the switch works, tape both corks in place.

Tip ✓ It is easier if you ask a friend to put the tape on while you hold the plastic round the cork.

The first switch works when it is tilted one way, which is fine for some projects. The switch shown here works when tilted two ways. Just add a second pair of paperclip contacts.

You could try different lengths of tube. What difference do you think this would make?

The switch below works when tilted in any direction. What difference do you think different sizes of box would make?

Use masking tape to fix the switch to things around you that move. Can you make the switch work when a door or one of your favourite things is moved? Can you hold the switch and climb over obstacles without setting it off?

Projects with moving parts could include the tilt switch to turn a circuit on automatically.

Think about using the tilt switches as starting points for design projects. The first switch could be built into a magic wand that lit up when pointed downwards at something. The box switch could be the start of a game design. Players could try to steer the ball round a track or maze without setting off an alarm.

27

A coin-operated switch

Make your own slot machine

Slot machines are used for lots of things including selling sweets, food, tickets and soft drinks. You can buy things when the shops are closed by putting money in a slot. What else are slot machines used for? What could they be used for?

The switch shown here works when a metal coin conducts electricity and closes the gap in the circuit. You can see the gap between the strips of foil. Here is how to make your own switch so that a buzzer, light or motor works when a coin is put in a slot. One use for a switch like this is to make collecting or saving money more fun. A well designed money box might make people put more money in the slot just to make it work!

You will need

- a box (like a shoe box) or cardboard to make one.
- a strip of corrugated cardboard
- kitchen foil
- a circuit (see pages 6-7)
- masking tape
- paper fasteners

kitchen foil

What to do

1. Choose (or make) a box that is big enough to hold your switch and collect the money.

2. Cut a strip of corrugated cardboard to the shape shown (above) and bend up the sides. The tubes inside the cardboard should run *along* the strip. Make the longest slide that will fit in your box.

3. Fix on two strips of foil using a glue stick. Smooth strips work best.

4. Staple the bare ends of a circuit tightly to the foil strips. You could add a capacitor (see page 9) to keep a light or buzzer on longer. Lay a coin on the switch to test it.

5. Fix your switch under a slot cut in the top of the box (get adult help). Make a gentle slope so that the coin will slide down slowly but without stopping.

Tip

Use masking tape to fix the switch until it works well, then fix with glue or paper fasteners.

A springy scoop made from a plastic bottle could be fixed above the switch. Make the holes in the scoop with a paper punch and fix it with paper fasteners.

When several coins are put in, their weight would tip the scoop, dumping the coins and switching the circuit on.

Getting ideas

You could design a money box where the switch turns on a light (see page 8). The light could be part of a picture on the box. A motor could make part of a picture spin. Clip-art pictures and word-processed writing from a computer could be used. You could design a box to collect money for a charity or good cause.

The basic switch can be changed in different ways. A hole could be cut in the slide so that coins that are too small will drop through into a reject box without turning the circuit on. A long slide will keep your circuit on for a longer time than a short one. If the slide was fixed level, one coin would keep the circuit on all the time. Could this be useful for some projects? You could have a different switch to turn the circuit off. Your switch and coin collecting box could be part of a bigger project. Could it turn on a motor to pull back a catch so that a door can be opened?

Index